gi Series

ORRIS

Water

The Corgi Series *Writing from Wales*

1 Dannie Abse, *Touch Wood*
2 Idris Davies, *A Carol for the Coalfield*
3 Mike Jenkins, *Laughter Tangled in Thorn*
4 *War*, an anthology edited by Dewi Roberts
5 Alun Richards, *Scandalous Thoughts*
6 Alun Lewis, *The Sentry*
7 Tony Curtis, *Considering Cassandra*
8 *Love*, an anthology edited by Dewi Roberts
9 Raymond Garlick, *The Delphic Voyage*
10 Rhys Davies, *Nightgown*
11 Sheenagh Pugh, *What If This Road*
12 *Places*, an anthology edited by Dewi Roberts
13 Leslie Norris, *Water*
14 T. H. Jones, *Lucky Jonah*
15 Paul Henry, *The Breath of Sleeping Boys*
16 *Work*, an anthology edited by Dewi Roberts
17 Harri Webb, *The Stone Face*
18 Geraint Goodwin, *The Shearing*
19 John Ormond, *Boundaries*
20 *Landscapes*, an anthology edited by Dewi Roberts
21 Glyn Jones, *The Common Path*
22 Gwyn Thomas, *Land! Land!*
23 Emyr Humphreys, *The Rigours of Inspection*
24 *Death*, an anthology edited by Dewi Roberts

The Corgi Series — Writing from Wales

Leslie Norris

Water

Poems and a story

Series editor

Meic Stephens

Emeritus Professor of Welsh Writing in English
University of Glamorgan

Carreg Gwalch Cyf.

ISBN: 0-86381-713-0

Cover design: Sian Parri
Carreg Gwalch Cyf. wishes to acknowledge the help of Martin Tinney Gallery, Cardiff (www.artwales.com) in supplying a slide of the artwork for the cover.

Logo design: Dylan Williams

First published in 2004 by
Carreg Gwalch Cyf., 12 Iard yr Orsaf, Llanrwst,
Wales LL26 0EH
☎ 01492 642031 🖷 01492 641502
books@carreg-gwalch.co.uk
website: www.carreg-gwalch.co.uk

Supported by an 'Arts for All' Lottery grant from the Arts Council of Wales

We wish to thank Seren for their co-operation in the production of this volume.

Contents

Leslie Norris

One of the most distinguished Welsh writers of his generation, Leslie Norris was born in Merthyr Tydfil in 1921. He was educated at Cyfarthfa Grammar School, Coventry Training College, where he trained as a teacher, and the University of Southampton. After being invalided out of the RAF, he was appointed headmaster of Westergate School in Chichester and then lecturer at the College of Education in Bognor Regis. In 1973, anxious to devote more time to his own writing, he accepted an invitation to be Visiting Professor at the University of Washington in Seattle, and so began a long association with American universities which has continued to the present. Since 1989 he has been Humanities Professor of Creative Writing at Brigham Young University in Utah.

The town of his birth figures prominently in Leslie Norris's poems and stories, though it is the old Merthyr, economically depressed but socially vibrant and brimming with colourful characters, that he looks back on with affection as a place in which it was ideal for a young poet to grow up. Beyond Cefn-coed lay the Brecon Beacons and the natural world of hills, streams and meadows which appear so often in his writing. The rural and industrial are seen at their most moving in 'Water', set on a hillside farm above Merthyr, and 'Elegy for David Beynon', about a teacher, a friend of the poet's, who died with his class in the Aberfan disaster of 1966. The elegiac note is also struck in poems for his contemporaries who died in the war.

But it is as a nature-poet that Leslie Norris excels. His observation of flora, fauna and aviana, whether in his native hills, or in the deserts of the American West, owes something to Edward Thomas, a poet whom he greatly admires and whose melancholy he shares. In poems such as 'Nightingales', 'Ransoms' and 'Mountains, Polecats, Pheasants' he celebrates the natural world with a fine understanding and without any hint of anthropomorphism or sentimentality. The efficacy of these poems has to do with the craftsmanship and command of language which are the hallmarks of his writing. These are 'well-made poems', with not a word out of place, their imagery meditated and honed, their metaphors carrying an emotional current that is never conspicuous but always an integral part of what the poet is saying. When he attempts the metaphysical it is not out of self-aggrandisement but from an ironic awareness of self that is both attractive and sometimes disturbing. Several, such as 'The Ballad of Billy Rose', have been anthologised more than a hundred times.

Leslie Norris is better-known in the USA than

he is in Wales, where he has not lived permanently since 1948. Although many of his poems remember the Wales of his boyhood and Carmarthenshire where he had, for a while, a small cottage from which he went fishing on the Teifi, his later poems reflect the looser contemporary styles of American poetry. His reputation in the United States was enhanced when he began contributing poems and stories to *The Atlantic Monthly* and *The New Yorker*, and since then he has won several prestigious prizes. The poems he has written in Maine and Utah are to be found in *Sequences* (1988) and *A Sea in the Desert* (1989), all of which are included in his *Collected Poems* (1996).

The same sensibilities and concerns inform Leslie Norris's short stories. They are a poet's stories, dealing with the numinous and the inexpressible in memorable ways. He has published two volumes of stories, namely *Sliding* (1976) and *The Girl from Cardigan* (1988), and his *Collected Stories* appeared in 1996. He has also published two books for children, *Merlin and the Snake's Egg* (1978) and *Albert and the Angels* (2000), both delightful evocations of childhood with a sense of fun and mischief, as well as a collection of poems for children, *Norris's Ark* (1988).

Leslie Norris is a complex man, proud of his calling as a poet, staunch in his friendships and unfailingly generous towards younger writers. If some critics have seen him as essentially a poet writing in the English Georgian tradition, and others have complained about his apparent lack of social awareness and his preoccupation with the Merthyr of his youth, he has stuck steadfastly to his last, content to remain 'at the edge of things', that mysterious land where the familiar and unfamiliar meet, and where his poems and stories have their abundant source.

Autumn Elegy

September. The small summer hangs its suns
On the chestnuts, and the world bends slowly
Out of the year. On tiles of the low barns
The lingering swallows rest in this timely

Warmth, collecting it. Standing in the garden,
I too feel its generosity; but would not leave.
Time, time to lock the heart. Nothing is sudden
In Autumn, yet the long, ceremonial passion of

The year's death comes quickly enough
As firm veins shut on the sluggish blood
And the numberless protestations of the leaf
Are mapped on the air. Live wood

Was scarce and bony where I lived as a boy.
I am not accustomed to such opulent
Panoply of dying. Yet, if I stare
Unmoved at the flaunting, silent

Agony in the country before a resonant
Wind anneals it, I am not diminished, it is not
That I do not see well, do not exult,
But that I remember again what

Young men of my own time died
In the Spring of their living and could not turn
To this. They died in their flames, hard
War destroyed them. Now as the trees burn

In the beginning glory of Autumn
I sing for all green deaths as I remember
In their broken Mays, and turn
The years back for them, every red September.

Early Frost

We were warned about frost, yet all day the
summer
Has wavered its heat above the empty stubble. Late
Bees hung their blunt weight,
Plump drops between those simplest wings, their
leisure
An ignorance of frost.
My mind is full of the images of summer
And a liquid curlew calls from alps of air;

But the frost has come. Already under trees
Pockets of summer are dying, wide paths
Of the cold glow clean through the stricken
thickets
And again I feel on my cheek the cut of winters
Dead. Once I awoke in a dark beyond moths
To a world still with freezing,
Hearing my father go to the yard for his ponies,

His hands full of frostnails to point their sliding
To a safe haul. I went to school,
Socks pulled over shoes for the streets' clear glass,
The early shops cautious, the tall
Classroom windows engraved by winter's chisel,
Fern, feather and flower that would not let the pale
Day through. We wrote in a cold fever for the
morning

Play. Then boys in the exulting yard, ringing
Boots hard on winter, slapped with their polishing
Caps the arrows of their gliding, in steaming lines
Ran till they launched one by one
On the skills of ice their frail balance,
Sliding through time with not a fall in mind,
Their voices crying freely through such shouting

As the cold divided. I slid in the depth
Of the season till the swung bell sang us in.
Now insidious frost, its parched grains rubbing
At crannies, moved on our skin.
Our fingers died. Not the warmth
Of all my eight wide summers could keep me
smiling.
The circle of the popping stove fell still

And we were early sped through the hurrying
dark.
I ran through the bitterness on legs
That might have been brittle, my breath
Solid, grasping at stabs of bleak
Pain to gasp on. Winter branched in me, ice cracked
In my bleeding. When I fell through the teeth
Of the cold at my haven door I could not see

For locked tears, I could not feel the spent
Plenty of flames banked at the range,
Nor my father's hands as they roughed the blue

Of my knees. But I knew what he meant
With the love of his rueful laugh, and my true
World unfroze in a flood of happy crying,
As hot on my cheek as the sting of this present

Frost. I have stood too long in the orderly
Cold of the garden, I would not have again the death
Of that day come unasked as the comfortless dusk
Past the stakes of my fences. Yet these are my
Ghosts, they do not need to ask
For housing when the early frost comes down.
I take them in, all, to the settled warmth.

Snow

The snow surprised us, coming
  When it did,
A sudden white swarm, humming
  Out of the long cloud.
Winter, with a cold deciduous voice,
Came briskly and purposefully upon us,

And our secure horizon
  Retracted
To a warm room's bounds. But children
  Swanked into the yard,
Their warm laughter twirling the prodigal snow
Into peaks, columns, ghosts – the afternoon glow

Was evergreen memory for them.
  So we all,
Warmed, went to the window, away from
  The surly fire. The tall
Snow fell, and thicket, hedge and fence,
Familiar limits all, burned so with snow's radiance

As to delight, renew us.
  And we saw,
Thirty years clearer our eyes,
  Ourselves, puffed round with scarves,
Like rainbow robins bounce on the stiff-legged snow,
Innocently singing with voices lost long ago.

The Ballad of Billy Rose

Outside Bristol Rovers Football Ground –
The date has gone from me, but not the day,
Nor how the dissenting flags in stiff array
Struck bravely out against the sky's grey round –

Near the Car Park then, past Austin and Ford,
Lagonda, Bentley, and a colourful patch
Of country coaches come in for the match
Was where I walked, having travelled the road

From Fishponds to watch Portsmouth in the Cup.
The Third Round, I believe. And I was filled
With the old excitement which had thrilled
Me so completely when, while growing up,

I went on Saturdays to match or fight.
Not only me; for thousands of us there
Strode forward eagerly, each man aware
Of tingling memory, anticipating delight.

We all marched forward, all except one man.
I saw him because he was paradoxically still,
A stone against the flood, face upright against us all,
Head bare, hoarse voice aloft, blind as a stone.

I knew him at once, despite his pathetic clothes;
Something in his stance, or his sturdy frame
Perhaps, I could even remember his name
Before I saw it on his blind-man's tray. Billy Rose.

And twenty forgetful years fell away at the sight.
Bare-kneed, dismayed, memory fled to the hub
Of Saturday violence, with friends to the Labour
Club,
Watching the boxing on a sawdust summer night.

The boys' enclosure close to the shabby ring
Was where we stood, clenched in a resin world,
Spoke in cool voices, lounged, were artificially
bored
During minor bouts. We paid threepence to go in.

Billy Rose fought there. He was top of the bill.
So brisk a fighter, so gallant, so precise!
Trim as a tree he stood for the ceremonies,
Then turned to meet George Morgan of Tirphil.

He had no chance. Courage was not enough,
Nor tight defence. Donald Davies was sick
And we threatened his cowardice with an
embarrassed kick.
Ripped across both his eyes was Rose, but we
were tough

And clapped him as they wrapped his blindness up
In busy towels, applauded the wave
He gave his executioners, cheered the brave
Blind man as he cleared with a jaunty hop

The top rope. I had forgotten that day
As if it were dead for ever, yet now I saw
The flowers of punched blood on the ring floor,
As bright as his name, I do not know

How long I stood with ghosts of the wild fists
And the cries of shaken boys long dead around me,
For struck to act at last, in terror and pity
I threw some frantic money, three treacherous
pence –

And I cry at the memory – into his tray, and ran,
Entering the waves of the stadium like a
drowning man.
Poor Billy Rose. God, he could fight
Before my three sharp coins knocked out his sight.

Picking Coal

I had thought until this late wind shook the wall
Winter had ended, but doors have banged all night
In the grumbling house,
Telling the sleepless about the entering weather.
A malignant cold, unwelcome, it turns the heart.

I remember a day like this, out of place in the warm
Young year. Frail sun licked the killed buds,
Ferns hung in the stopped
Threads of their fronds. Our breathing
unseasonably
Flowered, we were walking the weather away.

Weather is all summer for boys in their
confidence,
The sun inhabits them, their touch replenishes
What spoiled branches
They choose in their lucky vigour. But the land
So grown from our morning wishes, a blossoming
country,

Was struck by abrupt black winter in a killing
pyramid.
Our eyes could not fructify this. Death of the earth
Came in high cradles
From a harsh, close mine, on laborious wires,
Clumsily, inevitably. The dry axles' melancholy

Scraping squealed in the air like a disease of birds
And the heaped slag dropped, load on load,
Bones of the ripped pit's
Waste. Perched sliding, a man with his weak
Pick scratched among rattling for small knobs

Of lost coal, to warm in his sack. His long
Rags dragged in the dirt. He lived with winter.
Of his voice as he spoke
Across years and seasons through the cloud of his labour
I do not know, nor tell of his thin pale wrist

That no rubbed grime could strengthen. His decay grew
From the burned spoil where he stood. We were circled
By impregnable light and sun
And could not understand him, nor his sudden anger.
We offered him a cigarette from a rich packet,

But he refused, turning away with useless dignity.
It was golden David, so soon to die in exploding Europe,
Who lit up and smoked.
Now in my indolent, midsummer forties, hammocked in comfort,
It is this coldest wind disturbs, turning the heart.

Dead Boys

Here is the field, beneath two hundred houses,
Where the boy
Buried a dead bird.
He felt for it a small, universal sadness,
And gave it a birthday sixpence, all he had.
Among these urban gardens his remembered tears
Are old now, and real as the unravelling breezes
That thirty years blew all his grief to dry.

The pond was here, its arid grains are laid
Higher than boys
About these flimsy garages.
All night long, all one long winter night,
The old tin Fords stood with their headlights turned
On its drowning ice, thin as a ripped sheet,
Where the covered slider lay in his silent bubbles
And would not be found. His school cap wrongly
floated.

His name was known. The women sailed it
On gentle breath
Where they stood by the
Powerless cars in a darkness beyond rescue.
Gliding alone in the cold of a frozen death
He had not realised, the boy in his eyeless sight
Saw the face of the drowned, and held it
For simple mourning. He heard the desperate

Cursing of helpless fathers as weak ice kept
Them impotent.
Days are long to a boy;
Nights buried his foundered sadness in their tides
Till the black hulks slept in softness, as he slept.
Once he was thoughtless to an easy friend. The roads
Of summer led them away and they broke in a rough moment,
Never to meet again. It was here that he said goodbye

To his angular childhood. He walks the streets,
Their garish doors
Open to the field long gone,
And the grown man smiles as returning he meets,
In his eyed love, the cold, immortal children.
They run unblighted the green lanes of their time,
They laugh, their bright innocence unknown around them;
Here, where the field was, they live, the dead boys.

An Evening by the Lake

Well, let us admit it, I make
A pleasant picture here. A check
Overcoat, fresh from the cleaners,
Discreet suede shoes, (I use a wire brush),
Trouser-legs, that new bronze-green colour,
Just narrow enough for good taste.
I walk briskly, waving now and then and
Gently, a tweed hat.
Even my dog, unfashionable but
Successful, adds to my satisfaction.
She is obedient, but not servile.
On this grey evening, here at the edge
Of the lake and under the clouds,
She skips on the washed grass and is
Complacently white.
                                I have not lived
In the town for twenty years.

But walked this lakeside drive four times
A day when a boy, going to school
In a comic Gothic castle, built
For a fat iron-master. It turns
A stolid, limestone gaze down at
Me now.
                The park is quite deserted,
But for some poor boys, younger
Than I was, playing a thoughtless
Game a long way off. I watch them

Lift a great dressed stone, from
An old wall perhaps, stagger the few
Uneven yards to the water,
Then drop the huge thing in. I see
The little fountain of its drowning,
Then the slow circles spread. Boys' voices
Bounce to me over the resilient water.
Later I hear the stone's loud splash,
Much later.
                    Four of us on this lake,
Using two boats, once rowed for the price
Of their hire a furious race. Off
To a gasped start, we plunged our oars
For all our thin arms' worth,
Driving the clumsy prows through
Burst reflections of the full clouds
And green banks. When I lifted my
Dripping blade from the water, (Dan
Chanting our time), I could see behind
The lovely dimpling of its leaving
The liquid skin.
                              Then at last we stopped,
And called, our high voices skidding
Like flat, thrown stones over the resonant
Surface.
                    Just like these later voices,
And this younger water, which have
Entered the locked cellar of my mind,
Broken its seal, and let its darkness
Out.

So that I stand alone and
Bowed, on a scuffed, gravel path, in
A shabby park, my legs tired, my
Heart shaken, my jaunty clothes all
Wrong. All right, so my youth is dead.
And yes, those boys are gone.

The Strong Man

On my way to school I saw the man,
His little audience on the Square
Brought me abruptly running there.
Few on that boyhood afternoon
Had interest enough to spare,
Or money, to watch a rough tramp bare

To the waist perform his common tricks.
Incurious time had begun to wear
Haphazard patterns on his skin, to blur
The heavy flesh. He tore his packs
Of seedy cards, snapped through the air
The chains we'd thought as strong as care,

Leaving them empty on the ground.
Then, with a kind of wry despair,
He took a yard of iron bar,
Raised it, and brought it breaking down
On his own forearm. And over,
And over, boots kicking the floor,

The brisk tips sparking, until it had
Bent round his arm. His furious tonsure
Stung with sweat, his lips puffed lather,
The great ribs rasped. He stooped to the road
For his traps, his ripped shirt. We
Cheered his freedom: if such are free.

A Sense of History

Walking at random over the mountainous
moorland
With cry of curlew and wild mare's warning neigh
Held in an unhedged wind enough to knock your
head off,
At the bitter end of a swept and solitary day

I came at last to the shores of an incongruous water
Perched without purpose upon a mountain summit.
The eastern end was a shelving bank of stone
And the terrible wind blew stiff waves upon it.

And, head down along the edge, I could not help
notice
How all the long perimeter was similarly guarded
With single slices of stone, each patiently placed
Against the waves' water and into a crude mosaic.

Who dry-walled these shores? What men had
planned
These back-breaking banks and lived on the low
Secure island? (It is there still, and still the stone
Ungainly circles that were houses how long ago).

I only know that I was suddenly kneeling –
While over me flew the torn, unheeding froth –

And plugging with scales of stone the wave-worn
gaps,
Ten frozen fingers against the loud storm's tooth.

Then heading homeward through the embracing
marshland,
I faithfully found with quick and unearned skill
The hidden paths that led to the acquired valley,
Quite dry and hidden, away from wind, lake, hill.

Siencyn ap Nicolas upon his Death-bed

Well, we all come to it. Siencyn, listen
to their cringing philosophies as the tears glisten
in the eyes of your punctual mourners.
I wish a plague would fasten

Their plump hides to my stale bed!
But anger will never lift my head
again from this foul pillow.
I have learned tolerance, that soft word,

however unwillingly. It is one of my late,
one of my few, virtues. I hate
the hypocrite who takes a pleasure
in his honesty. Many a desolate

truth I've undone with a kind
lie. And hope to be forgiven. We can't stand
all kinds of truth. If God calls for my
account I must ask Him to turn a blind

eye to truth's ledgers, for there
I have no credit. When I spare
time for plain speaking I make sure
I'm not believed. There is a wild humour

in the accidental, savage truth I use
that makes it fictional. Old men can choose

a kind of general truth that turns to wisdom
being void of malice. Not my way. But I'd not lose

a chance nobility I might, like a burr,
have picked on any casual road or moor
I've walked in my time. I'll not claim
merit for it. God's will. Found, not worked for.

Straight paths were never mine. When I was young
I let the hot blood take me where it stung.
God's doing, surely? He must know
His beautiful youths. I felt the sun

rise in my flushed veins, for the hot south
of life was in me and the songs my mouth
made then were many and easy. All roads
were mine for the laughing, and taking a breath

was like drinking wine. Yes, I remember
days when my five electric senses burned so clear
that I saw pale rainbows circumscribe the moon,
heard audible butterflies beat upon the air.

And the people I knew! A bright harmless
young man has friends everywhere. I witness
now that there was warmth on all the roads
for fifty miles and laughter in the villages

when I entered. And gave no thought to.
What's thought when the eager young are at their
play?
Twin-faced I followed every tempting bend,
alone on the ecstatic hills, or roaring in company.

I eased my ways through the lanes, and the taverns
knew me well. Slept nights in the tall ferns
and laughed in the dark. Groped awake
in the smart mornings and ran to the barns.

Then, one evening, I felt myself taken,
my legs not my own, afraid and shaken
by an apprehension of power beyond
all I could guess, to a path on the mountain

where climbing through rowan and bracken –
I see it all still – I came to a broken
and absolute crest. In the world beneath
the bright farms went to sleep, and the moon

began in splendour her processional ceremony.
This was how I was called to my craft. I knew
from that moment that all must be seen and said,
that words not mine would seem to be

mine. I climbed the hill alone and left alone,
yet all around me tree and beast and stone
moved as I moved. The wary twigs stared.

Feathers of birds rooted at my shoulder-bone.

So I have walked the hills for what might have
been lost.
I have seen the sun walk drenched out of the mist
of early morning, and dance on the hill-top. I have
been old as a stone the lichen has soundlessly
kissed

and known all enduring life in inanimate things.
I have left my body and grasped the soft rungs
of the air. Trees and grasses live in me,
through me the long-dead sing again their songs.

Is this not Heaven? Yes, it is mine.
And therefore true. I was always one of Aristotle's
men
for whom the ideal good is never pure
abstraction. We make our images warm, human,

looking on our own distortions kindly.
But I'll not reject any sly hope of a friendly
Heaven to come. Not that I've earned it.
No, I must enter by invitation only.

Now it is autumn and pigeons flock to the fields,
bald listless blackbirds lurk in the muddy laurels
and the heavy geese drive their high, frail wedges
into an iron sky. The birds are restless,

as I am restless, held in a filthy
cage of flesh, an old, sick man in a healthy
place, living his last on a rich son's
ready charity. Now in this wealthy

home I lie on a generous bed and feel
my life slide. I have sent away the girl
who came to read to me. To the young
nothing is simple. Why should my carrion smell

infect her innocence? Or my withered arm
misuse her compassion? Outside my room
the black weepers await my last
action. The ominous birds fly home.

And I must make my one way from
this shrivelled house of bones. I'll not welcome
Death, except in the way of courtesy.
I've loved in the world too long. But let him come.

Nightingales

1

My namesake, old Bill Norris, standing beneath a
tree
So bitterly gnarled he might have grown from it,
stopped
Talking to listen, lifted eyes dayblue and delighted,
And laughed a silent pleasure. 'There's a good
many,'
He said, 'Walks past as close as you and never
hears her,
Though she sings as bright in the hot noon as any
night.'
Two feet above his head the dun bird pulsed and
lilted.
It was in this village and perhaps for this same bird
I lay awake the whole of one miraculous darkness.
She sang so close to my house I could have touched
Her singing; I could not breathe through the
aching silences.
And for nights after, hunched among pillows, I
grabbed
At any sleep at all, hearing the nightingale
Hammer my plaintive rest with remorseless melody.
Full of resented ecstasy, I groaned nightlong in my
bed.

2

Or driving one Sunday morning in Maytime Hampshire
On our way to a christening in one of the villages,
We stopped on Steep Hill, the road climbing headily upwards.
In the first warm air of the year we looked down on the
Trees, unmoving and full in the freshness of their leaves.
There were eight nightingales, eight, they filled the valley
With sobbing, the cataracts of their voices fell
Erratically among the splendid beeches. Open-eyed
We stood on the lip of the hill, while near and far
The water-notes of their singing grew faint, were lost almost,
Answered and redoubled near at hand, trailed
Dropping sadly down the valley-sides, struck purely out
With sound round notes into the listening morning.
We were still with music, as the day was. That we were late
For the christening was to the credit of those nightingales.

3

When I was very young my father took me from
bed,
Dressed me in haste, and we walked into the night.
Winter was so long gone I had forgotten darkness.
We went by paths which in daylight knew me well,
But now were strange with shadow. It was not
long
Before we came to the wood where the
nightingale sang,
The unbelievable bird who lived in the stories
Of almost my every book. Would it sing, would it
sing?
I thought the wood was full of silent listeners.
I do not remember it singing. My father carried
me home,
My head rolling back on its stalk at every measure
Of his deep stride, and all I have brought back
From that long night are the fixed stars reeling.
It is the poet's bird, they say. Perhaps I took it home,
For here I am, raising my voice, scraping my
throat raw again.

Finding Gold

From his house each day the child moves to school
Through a deliberate ceremony. He is obsessed
By a chosen maze, marking his ritual
With clear jumps over long stones full
Of inescapable bad luck, then a stick's rattle
Briskly along twenty-three exact bars of tall
Fence outside the bus station; the road crossed
Here, always. His frail, unswerving rule
Is to impose order on a chaotic world.

Pressed by his abiding route, he mounts the stone
Parapet. One step to the edge and, elate
With danger, coldly he stares down at
The diminished water. Freckled mallows fret
At the shallow runs. Slowly, slowly now, must
He turn and saunter with rehearsed arrogance the lane
Through the sagging garages, slack doors on the yawn.
He will not move his head when shadows threaten,
Nor falter a slid inch from his restricted cobbles.

But here in a sunny gap between two sheds
Is a circle of stone seats, loosely deserted.
Black as police stand the rough walls, the gamblers
Are running down tittering alleys, their cards
Scattered as windfalls, their copper bets

Spilled in fallen coils. The quick child
Hurries deep coins into the crannies of his pockets
And breaks for school. All safe custom run wild,
He laughs in the tumble of the anonymous
playground.

All day he sat in school, full of pennies
To his round eyes. He thought without moving
Of springing circles of stone standing inches
Outside his orderly magic, and knew for us
All, one step from broken practice the spread gold
lies,
In the green lanes of absence. Are his coins living?
Does he stride on the mapless hills where the
gamblers'
Dust is lifted? Is he stumping his trodden roads
With an old day turning, stupidly turning?

Water

On hot summer mornings my aunt set glasses
On a low wall outside the farmhouse,
With some jugs of cold water.
I would sit in the dark hall, or
                    Behind the dairy window,
Waiting for children to come from the town.

They came in small groups, serious, steady,
And I could see them, black in the heat,
Long before they turned in at our gate
To march up the soft, dirt road.
                    They would stand by the wall,
Drinking water with an engrossed thirst. The dog

Did not bother them, knowing them responsible
Travellers. They held in quiet hands their bags
Of jam sandwiches, and bottles of yellow fizz.
Sometimes they waved a gratitude to the house,
                    But they never looked at us.
Their eyes were full of the mountain, lifting

Their measuring faces above our long hedge.
When they had gone I would climb the wall,
Looking for them among the thin sheep runs.
Their heads were a resolute darkness among ferns,
                    They climbed with unsteady certainty.
I wondered what it was they knew the mountain
                                                            had.

They would pass the last house, Lambert's where
A violent gander, too old by many a Christmas,
Blared evil warning from his bitten moor,
Then it was open world, too high and clear
        For clouds even, where over heather
The free hare cleanly ran, and the summer sheep.

I knew this; and I knew all summer long
Those visionary gangs passed through our lanes,
Coming down at evening, their arms full
Of cowslips, moon daisies, whinberries, nuts,
        All fruits of the sliding seasons,
And the enormous experience of the mountain

That I who loved it did not understand.
In the summer, dust filled our winter ruts
With a level softness, and children walked
At evening through golden curtains scuffed
        From the road by their trailing feet.
They would drink tiredly at our wall, talking

Softly, leaning, their sleepy faces warm for home.
We would see them murmur slowly through our
                                                stiff
Gate, their shy heads gilded by the last sun.
One by one we would gather up the used jugs,
        The glasses. We would pour away
A little water. It would lie on the thick dust,
                                gleaming.

Now the House Sleeps

Now the house sleeps among its trees,
Those charcoal scratches on the sky's
Good morning, and I walk the lane
That all night long has quietly gone
Down the cold hill, and quietly up
Until it reached that darkened top
Where the shrill light of a short day
Begins again the frozen glow

Of winter dawn. I contemplate
The wealth of day that has to wait
The recognition of my eye.
Reality is what we see,
Or what my senses all achieve;
What they believe, so I believe.
Around, the ring of hills wears light
Of morning like a steel helmet

And below them, in the brown
Cleansing of its floods, runs down
The brawling river. Now the owl,
That all night held its floating call
Over the terrified hedges, climbs
In clumsy blindness to the elm's
Black safety, there flops down,
A comfortable, daylight clown;

And little animals of night
Retire as silent as the light
To sleeping darkness. Closing the door,
I leave the white fields desert for
The loss of my descriptive eye.
The sunlit measures of the day
Are unregarded. I cut bread,
Knowing the world untenanted.

And yet, although my sight must stop
At the solid wall, a world builds up,
Feature by feature, root by root,
The soft advance of fields, daylight
Reaching west in the turn of life,
Personal, created world, half
Ignorant, half understood. And I
Complete from faulty memory

And partial complexities of sense
Those images of experience
That make approximate rivers move
Through the wrong world in which I live,
Or chart a neat uncertainty
Down major roads to Nowhere City;
But at the edge of what I know
The massed, appalling forests grow.

Through the long night the rough trucks grind
The highways, gears ripping blind,
Headlights awash on the tarmac;
All night long metallic traffic,
Racks of concrete, rams of girders,
Heavy oppression of cities
Forced by a crude growling. Yet all
Are Plato's shadows on the wall,

Noises drifting among shadows,
Shadows dying among echoes,
While clear eternities of light
Shine somewhere on the perfect world
We cannot know. My shadowed field
Lies in its flawed morning, and dirt
Falls in the slow ditches. Sunrise,
And the house wakes among its trees.

Postcards from Wales

Whenever I think of Wales, I hear the voices
Of children calling, and the world shrinks to the
span
Of a dozen hills. As I wander to sleep
The water voices of the streams begin.

Green air, the truthful winds shall sing you
Over the lean hill and the melancholy
Valley of childhood.

We swam free rivers that our tongues resembled,
We lit the summer dark with lazy fire
At the waterside. And when silence fell
It was not passing time we grew to hear,

Winter. The blind lake turns its solid
Eye to the snowcloud. In the village
The doors are fast, the chimneys fat with coalsmoke

But the world changing, the tall hills tumbling,
The universe of terraces waning small.
Beyond brief rivers we heard the urgent sea
Knock to come in. It was a miracle

The spent salmon drops tail first to the sea.
His lank sides heave. His exhausted eye
Turns away for another year.

Of our own discovering. Whenever I think of Wales,
I think of my leaving, the farewell valleys letting go
And the quick voices falling far behind in the dust
Off the dry tips. And I think of returning, too,

Cae Gwair is spotted with orchises;
The earth, finding its own rich heat,
Releases it in little purple columns.

On some afternoon warm and loving, to a handful
Of fields by Teifi river and a cottage blind
With waiting. I know those rough, wind-turning
Walls were made in childhood, I know my mind

In September the cold ponies
Return from the high moor. They kick
Down the tottering stones and relish the gardens.

Invents the long, immaculate weather of a year
Unpredictable as truth. But the river's voice
Is forever filling the valley, filling it,
And remembered voices are underneath my
windows.

A Girl's Song

Early one morning
As I went out walking
I saw the young sailor
Go fresh through the fields.
His eye was as blue as
The sky up above us
And clean was his skin
As the colour of shells.

O where are you going,
Young sailor, so early?
And may I come with you
A step as you go?
He looked with his eye
And I saw the deep sea-tombs,
He opened his mouth
And I heard the sea roar.

And limp on his head
Lay his hair green as sea-grass
And scrubbed were his bones
By the inching of sand.
The long tides enfolded
The lines of his body
And slow corals grow
At the stretch of his hand.

I look from my window
In the first light of morning
And I look from my door
At the dark of the day,
But all that I see are
The fields flat and empty
And the black road run down
To Cardigan town.

Fishing the Teifi

Left bank and right,
I've fished this water since first light,
Pitching my early spinners
Into the river's mirrors,
Feeling the hook sink
Minutely, then I'd check, and bring it to the bank.

It was enough at first
To know the thrown perfection of each cast,
My eight-foot, fibreglass flinger
Growing from my hand, a finger
To set exactly down
My teal and black, mallard and claret, or coachman.

But I've had nothing on
All morning nor the longer afternoon.
For all his hunched attention
The empty heron's flown,
And now the soft-whistling otter
Glides his long belly into the blackening water.

From the bleak dark the hiss
Of a harsh wind turns my face
Down like a sheet, telling me to go.
But sleep tonight I know
Will not shut out this river, nor the gleam
Of big fish, sliding up to hook onto my dream.

Dog

On a field like a green roof
Pitched by the sea wind
A patch of uncertain sheep
Each poised on pointed hoof
Ready for running
Stare at the coiled bitch
Alert for their turning

And stamp as she sidles
And freezes. They pick
At the steep field, they back,
Disturbing the nervous edge
Of their fleecy circle.
Slowly the bitch inches
And with a rush

Channels the stunned run.
They stream in a prim file
Through the one marked gap
In the leaning hedge,
And Fan, tongue sideways lolling
Ushers them softly through.
Adrift on the stiff hill

The cold shepherd does not even watch them.

October in the Lane

October in the lane, and the thin harebells,
Ghosts of their deep Augusts, pine in the hedges.
Puffed leaves thicken the crawling ditches
And tired wasps labour in the air,

Heavy with dying. Our trees prepare
The black calligraphies of winter, we strip
Our fields for the frost fire. Now roses drop
From the wall their falls of petals

And cheat my eyes with snowflakes. Smells
Of marauding weather come coldly in with the dark.
I remember a spring of snow that fell without mark
On my head and white hurry as I thudded for home

And we laughed to see how soon I became,
In a falling minute, a seven year old, white-haired man.
In the kitchen mirror I watched the quick years run
From the warm, and I wiped from my head

The unready white my April time pretended.
So many weathers have spread their tempers near me
That empty winters stretch behind my mirror
And the keenest razor will not shift their snowfalls.

Old Voices

First the one bell, heavy, behind it
Centuries of controlled certainty, swung
With an enormous sound past
The kneeling city; it is the first
Heard stone in an architecture of ringing.
And sung in at built intervals, at
The joint of locked structure, the voice
Of the second bell. The foundation is

Set on unimpeded air. An age
Of cut stone and iron – those old
Technologies – has its immense medieval
Tongues bellowing again. Now all
The small bells filigree and stretch
A long nave in the ear and a pulled
Spire of sailing clamour. Resonant
Cathedrals of listening are launched

On the open day. But bells are not
Peaceful; are arrogant with the complete
World of their origin. Think, imagine,
In the clack of swords they began,
Short on their own shields the flat beat
Struck, so that erratic courage set
Hard in the metal; then the high edge,
Turning in the urgency of the charge,

Rang through the heads of wives
At their keen mourning. Hacking the bent
Angles of helmets, rough blades cracked again
The wombs that bore these splintered heads
In their early down. From such sounds,
From the held quiet after, the brazen
Complexities of the loud tower grew.
There was time for the patterns of victory,

And space on the fat plains of grain
For building of flawless bells. The lost
In their slate hills had tongues only,
Grew old in the slow labour
Of changing myths. Through the mist
Of altering voices their stories spun,
Through generations of telling. Spiral
Images from the belfries, the metal

Confections of chiming, are not
For the mountains. Old men tell
Of an impermanent peace, a fragile
Faith is passed through narrative
Villages in syllables of live
Whispers. Foolish now to regret
Centuries of locked exile. It happened.
We have heads full of easy legend

And elegies like the cold sun
Of treeless autumn. I carry
Such tunes in my head like the thin
Silence the bells hang in. But from
These reaching fields my surnamed
Fathers came, the great cathedrals
Counted them. I walk their lanes,
My shoes cover the concave stones

Worn by their slow tolling.
If I speak with the quick brooks
Of the permanent hills, in my saying
See hordes of the dark tribes stand,
Their faces hidden, my hand
In its perfect glove of skin holds
Other ghosts. We step the streets
Uneasily, disturbed by bells.

Barn Owl

Ernie Morgan found him, a small
Fur mitten inexplicably upright,
And hissing like a treble kettle
Beneath the tree he'd fallen from.
His bright eye frightened Ernie,
Who popped a rusty bucket over him
And ran for us. We kept him
In a backyard shed, perched
On the rung of a broken deck-chair,
Its canvas faded to his down's biscuit.
Men from the pits, their own childhood
Spent waste in the crippling earth,
Held him gently, brought him mice
From the wealth of our riddled tenements,
Saw that we understood his tenderness,
His tiny body under its puffed quilt,
Then left us alone. We called him Snowy.

He was never clumsy. He flew
From the first like a skilled moth,
Sifting the air with feathers,
Floating it softly to the place he wanted.
At dusk he'd stir, preen, stand
At the window-ledge, fly. It was
A catching of the heart to see him go.
Six months we kept him, saw him
Grow beautiful in a way each thought

His own knowledge. One afternoon, home
With pretended illness, I watched him
Leave. It was daylight. He lifted slowly
Over the Hughes's roof, his cream face calm,
And never came back. I saw this;
And tell it for the first time,
Having wanted to keep his mystery.

And would not say it now, but that
This morning, walking in Slindon woods
Before the sun, I found a barn owl
Dead in the rusty bracken.
He was not clumsy in his death,
His wings folded decently to him,
His plumes, unruffled orange,
Bore flawlessly their delicate patterning.
With a stick I turned him, not
Wishing to touch his feathery stiffness.
There was neither blood nor wound on him,
But for the savaged foot a scavenger
Had ripped. I saw the sinews.
I could have skewered them out
Like a common fowl's. Moving away
I was oppressed by him, thinking
Confusedly that down the generations
Of air this death was Snowy's
Emblematic messenger, that I should know
The meaning of it, the dead barn owl.

Burning the Bracken

When summer stopped, and the last
Lit cloud blazed tawny cumulus
Above the hills, it was the bracken

Answered; its still crests
Contained an autumn's burning.
Then, on an afternoon of promised

Cold, true flames ripped
The ferns. Hurrying fire, low
And pale in the sun, ran

Glittering through them. As
Night fell, the brindle
Flambeaux, full of chattering

We were too far to hear, leapt
To the children's singing.
'Fire on the mountain,' we

Chanted, who went to bed warmed
By joy. But I would know that fires
Die, that the cold sky holds

Uneasily the fronds and floating
Twigs of broken soot, letting
Them fall, fall now, soft

As darkness on this white page.

Mountains Polecats Pheasants

I have seen these hills closed
By impassive winter, and stood,
Banging my arms, on the last
Cold yard of road before snow
Came down on memory, the way

Strange as Asia. In summer,
Loss of the travelled sun drops
A bulk of mountain into shadow
Deep enough to lose a town in,
And scared cars, smaller, run

For the lit valleys. I thought
The mountains safe in my mind
From all revelation, but
Had never before driven late
Their cleft passes. Midnight

Had left the road as I climbed
The foothills, the car slotted
Behind headlights and the warmed
Engine humming at gradients
Above the farms. Fenceless.

The ponies slept, their fetlocks
Still, their wild skulls fallen
To stone. It was a dark

Palpable as ice on those
Stone ranges. On a blunt rise,

Where the wind scorched black
The stump hawthorns and hedge
Grass bent thick in the shock
Of wind, I saw in my lights
Such tiny brilliances. Not cats',

Not foxes' eyes shone colder.
Cutting the engine, I softened
Downroad to where they were:
Polecats, the mother stiff
With instinct, her emeralds of

Sight full on my pointing;
Her five young, caught
In a lesson of hunting.
Fear moved her, sliding her
Flat as oil and under

The light; but her innocents
Stayed, weaving their baby heads.
They mewed, their sweet throats
Tame as milk. Their gentling
Cries showed me their kindling,

Blind in a hard nest under
The piled rocks. I knew the slit

Of their eyes against the thunder
Of light. I wished for them
A lenient dark and safe home.

Last year, in true daylight,
At a faultless eighty on
Other roads, it was soft
Death I passed. A bag, burst
Cushion, cracked feathers drift-

ing after smash, the hen
Pheasant lay. There was no
Terror in that sight. When
She was puffed to one side
In a bundle of snapped

Shafts, she lay roundly where
She fell. The slow blood
Failed to mark the air
For her, but in the fallen
Wreaths of her plumes ran

Her dozen chicks, no more
Than hours after hatching.
I could not catch them, nor
Could I harry them to safe
Hiding before rough

Death wiped their brief
Smudges under the wheels
Of cars. The stuff of
The roads, oil, grit, fine
Dust, absorbed their stain.

There was nothing to show for them,
Though they came from the perfect
Eggs this mother alone could form.
When she died, feathers hung
A week in the hedge, turning

Black in the hot exhausts.
I know that my polecats
Are old now in the deaths
Of their needed victims,
I know there are cold times.

When the fields whistle
In fear of them, the grass
Thickens as they ripple
Through, tearing murder. Yet
I would have had them meet,

Polecats and pheasants, on
Their common hills. I would
Have had them live, and
In a night more terrible
Than the terrible fall

Of shadow or winter over
These mountains I close again,
Let the truth turn clear
For them, the last whimper
Of it, true hunted, true hunter.

July the Seventh

Drugged all day, the summer
Flagged in its heat, brutal
Weather sullen as brass.
There was no comfort in darkness.
Hotter than breath we lay

On beds too warm for moving,
Near open windows. Full of
Spaces the house was, walls
Fretting for a brisk air.
A door slammed flat in its

Loud frame, banging us awake.
Wind was bringing in the storm.
Quick switches of whipped light
Flicked the rooftops, made shadowless
The ends of rooms. The stopped clock

Marked the lightning. I got up
Heavily, shut the house against
Thunder. Rain was a long time
Coming, then sparse drops, stinging
Like metal, hit the bricks, the hot

Pavements. When it sweetened
To plenty, the streets tamed it,
Flowed it in pipes and conduits,

Channelled it underground through
Stony runnels. The rain brought

So faint a smell of hay I searched
My mind for it, thinking it memory.
I lay freshly awake on the cool sheets,
Hearing the storm. Somewhere, far off,
Cut grass lay in files, the hay spoiling.

Shadows

(for John Ormond)

In the night world, it was
The river was black.
Not reeds at the water's
Edge, streaked with darkness,
Not the dim coldness, back
Under the trees, were black.

It was the river. And
He lay in his smooth pool,
Slack in it, blind
In it, fanning the sand
Under him, with his tail.
He did not hear at all

Quick whispers on the bank,
Nor the furtive launching
From the brink
Of the river. His roof broke
In a small furrow along
The bend, in the swing

Of the current. He did
Not know. He lay safe
In his size, the cold
Strength that none could
Be stronger. With a flick of
His neck he could rip off

The cheap lures cast for him,
He could bull the water
Until it boiled after him,
Even out of heavy calm,
Even out of warm summer
Glaze, with his bludgeoning shoulder.

But now he lay in the balm
Tide, under the boat sailed
Secretly to kill him,
And he did not know. For him
Alone the darkness held
Its breath over river and field.

When the light slashed
The water, white torch
Pointed at him, lanced
At him, he held clenched
Against fright in the touch
Of light. He did not flinch

From lick of light, the sun
Itself in the healthy day
Did not disturb him when
He rolled in his weight down
Bending falls. But now
It was the shadow

Of his fear hung under
Him, black, ominous, pressed
Flat against gravel. Whether
The mincing river
Trembled it, or greed
Quivered the hawk boat,

He knew in his skin
The hunger of its waiting.
And he turned quietly in
From the edge of light, watching
It turn with him, cling
To him; and it ran

Behind him and under
Him as he ran
From the closing floor
Of the river.
His shadow ran
As close as the pain

Of his terror, and now
He swam furiously from
It, up, from it, away
From it, into
The clear light of freedom.
And the murderous gaff saved him.

And our faces stared red,
Reflecting
His gashed blood.
The shadow of his killing,
Sunk under mortal stain,
Waits other lights, other salmon.

Bridges

Imagine the bridge launched, its one foot
Clamped hard on bedrock, and such grace
In its growth it resembles flying, is flight
Almost. It is not chance when they speak
Of throwing a bridge; it leaves behind a track
Of its parallel rise and fall, solid
In quarried stone, in timber, in milled
Alloy under stress. A bridge is

The path of flight. A friend, a soldier,
Built a laughable wartime bridge over
Some unknown river. In featureless night
He threw from each slid bank the images
Of his crossing, working in whispers, under
Failing lamps. As they built, braced spars
Bolted taut the great steel plugs, he hoped
His bridge would stand in brawny daylight,
complete,

The two halves miraculously knit. But
It didn't. Airily they floated above
Midstream, going nowhere, separate
Beginnings of different bridges, offering
The policies of inaction, neither coming
Nor going. His rough men cursed, sloped off,
Forded quite easily a mile lower.
It was shallow enough for his Land Rover.

I have a bridge over a stream. Four
Wooden sleepers, simple, direct. After rain,
Very slippery. I rarely cross right over,
Preferring to stand, watching the grain
On running water. I like such bridges best,
River bridges on which men always stand,
In quiet places. Unless I could have that other,
A bridge launched, hovering, wondering where to
land.

Elegy for David Beynon

David, we must have looked comic, sitting
there at next desks; your legs stretched
half-way down the classroom, while
my feet hung a free inch above

the floor. I remember, too, down
at The Gwynne's Field, at the side
of the little Taff, dancing with
laughing fury as you caught

effortlessly at the line-out, sliding
the ball over my head direct to
the outside-half. That was Cyril
Theophilus, who died in his quiet

so long ago that only I, perhaps,
remember he'd hold the ball one-handed
on his thin stomach as he turned
to run. Even there you were careful

to miss us with your scattering
knees as you bumped through
for yet another try. Buffeted
we were, but cheered too by our

unhurt presumption in believing
we could ever have pulled you down.
I think those children, those who died
under your arms in the crushed school,

would understand that I make this
your elegy. I know the face you had,
have walked with you enough mornings
under the fallen leaves. Theirs is

the great anonymous tragedy one word
will summarise. Aberfan, I write it
for them here, knowing we've paid to it
our shabby pence, and now it can be stored

with whatever names there are where
children end their briefest pilgrimage.
I cannot find the words for you, David. These
are too long, too many; and not enough.

i.m. James Chuang, MB, BS, MRCS, RN

(died April 23 1978, aged 25)

Last Thursday morning, watching a haul of barges
tug their blunt ropes under Chelsea Bridge,
I saw two swallows, hot from Africa,
flick and scream across the delighted river.
First of the warming year, emblem and omen,
one for each day of all that remained of your life.

Jim, I can't understand how anyone as young
and generous could go so swiftly into death.
It was good that afternoon, walking in Hyde Park,
watching the little goldeneye, pair by pair
in meticulous black and white, bobbing
on the cold Serpentine. To see them dive!

They'd slip under the water so casually,
without taking breath, without preparation
slide into the silence, longer and deeper,
until we couldn't see them. They all came back.
One by one all popped up from their underworld,
out of their darkness. Small London children,

playing with grandparents, clapped their hands
at each abrupt return. We spoke of your work
at Greenwich Hospital, the Seamen's Hospital
down by the widening Thames, and I was startled
by the wholeness of your compassion, your serious
tolerance. You were a chosen man. Somewhere

away from my awareness you had come of age.
And since then I've been finding it difficult
to remember you as a small boy, that brush-head,
the apricot-coloured child who would bring his
reading book, or that older one in Christ's
Hospital blue, alert, smiling, always eager.

On Thursday afternoon I knew you the full man,
conscious of healing, able to keep death at bay
down there near the river. Images of your childhood
were not wanted. You had become my contemporary,
although you were young enough to clap your hands
with the children, and I stand in an older body.

(Conscious of certain wreck, Jim, I had meant
to ask about arthritis, how my fingers stiffen;
but had not thought to know the pain of knocking
these words out.) To think a starling's nest,
untidy tangle of instinct pressed messily
into an air vent, could have killed you.

Anger meant little to you. If I am angry
it is a futility you must allow me now.
Two Canada geese, those heavy winter birds,
grey on a grey sky, beat overhead, trailing
silence behind their ponderous flying.
A cold evening has come back to the country.

Islands off Maine

(for Charles and Jeannie Wadsworth)

1

One man hammering
From his home on crevices
Shatters the darkness
Over the islands.

Dawn moves briskly
Among the rugosas
And the harbour lights take back
Their shaken images.

Water smooth as claws
Holds its silent traps;
On the visible tide
Floats huge America.

2

In the spring of the year eight ospreys
Flew over the island; smaller birds
Squalled at them, pollack and mackerel
Spun in their flustered shoals beneath

The seahawks' wings. Six flew on
To cull more northern waters; two stayed,
Perched much on trees, and hunted
Entirely in flight, circling. Hung

Two hundred feet above what fish
They chose; and fell, the vertical
Steep plunge between their own
Talons, then the consummate grab.

For surface fish they disturbed
No more than the sea's lace before
Flicking away water and taking off,
But can dive a yard into the packed

Ocean, feet braced thick against impact,
The toes lined with spicules, the claws
Stiff, and the whole battered water suddenly
Over their five-foot wings. They close

Their nostrils against the salt entry
And never fail. A sodden flap off
The surface they shiver away droplets,
Carry their fish head first, a torpedo.

All summer we saw their young in the
Flattened spruce top, all day we heard
Their mewling hunger, until they flew
On the cooling air, down the long coast.

3

And on the point one day,
Mist flattening the island,
I met the mad boy.

Brambles had torn his jeans,
His fingers were harsh as carrots,
Waterbeads dropped in his bull's curls.

His voice would not behave,
His skull was echoing and
The mist was behind his eyes.

'What d'you like about Maine,
Hey, what d'you like about it?'
Screaming like a blue jay

Mountains, I told him, mostly
The mountains, but the sea too.
His joy was terrible, he hopped

In the gritty pebbles, he slapped
His laughing over the vague beach.
'Sure, there were mountains Monday

– today there ain't mountains!'
The island stopped where he pointed,
His hand wiped out Mount Cadillac.

'When you leaving, why don't you?
Why don't you leave? If you knew
The people here, you'd leave today!'

He moved away, was a stone, a
Post, a shape among shifting
Shapes, a slow uncertainty.

Unseen gulls jeered from the rocks.
Pewter light off the water
Faded when I hit the dirt path.

4

Pink Harding, born on the island,
Counts time in decades. Her chair
Rocks away anything smaller.

In all her years the sea has not stopped
Running. Each tide piles higher the granite
Pebbles, the red granite and the grey.

Hummingbirds visit her white phlox.
She is glad to hear this, but has seen
Them before. She is up since dawn.

We shout down her deafness, but scar tissue
Rubs at her eyes. She no longer braids

The tied rugs for which she's famous.

'Some I had ten dollars for!' she still
Marvels, 'And not always the best ones.'
They're heirlooms now, hang in museums.

She speaks of her father, that good man,
Then sits up, lifts one hand in pride,
'My grandfather was a full-blooded Englishman.'

5

Four white posts and a length of chain
Enclose the burial ground. Its stillness
Is twelve low headstones among the spruce.
You could walk past it, your head down

Against mosquitoes, and not see it.
Here lie the old, in the amplitude
And honour of their longevity: Capt.
Thos. Manchester, AE 92 yrs 3 mos;

Hannah, his Wife, AE 87 yrs 5 mos;
And nine others. But Gilman U. Stanley,
A boy, he sailed east and north
Out of Cranberry, past Novia Scotia,

In the temperate summer of 1861, watched
With his living eyes the Atlantic
Shake back the pack ice off Cape Breton.
All his life he'd seen harbour porpoise,

But now he called the finback whale,
The humpback whale, the minke and right
Whales as they rolled and mountained in their
Buoyant schools across the Cabot Strait.

Rich waters! O rich, destructive waters!
Working northward, never far from landfall,
They kept Anticosti to larboard, and Cape Whittle
And Little Mecatina Island; and saw on the right

The grave Newfoundland headlands where they
Should be, reaching on June 16 the Strait
Of Belle Isle. Where the boy at once went
Down. The sea took him, pressed flat

His agile breath, swam him among rocks
In water blue as ice, broke him in deep
Currents so that he lolled boneless.
Son of Jonathan R. and Irene Stanley,

AE 16 yrs 8 mos 28 dys. Each year the scrub,
The quiet moss, the little evergreens, move
Like a slow green tide on his empty grave,
Break on his headstone, and the other headstones.

6

water bell
sea's angelus
anchored edge of rock
and steep of water

toll for us

audible hanging wave
simple element
mouth of the round tide
storm's voice

toll for us
in our leaving

water tongue
clapper and safe hammer
sea's elegy and sound

celebrate our passing

toll for us

These Hills, These Woods

Who comes out of these hills, these woods,
from the small white house in the hollow,
from the summer river between ferns?
Who travels the rough lanes worn

by the stumbling dung-cart? They carry
among the bundled clutter of clothes and pans
and the rattle of what is portable
the whole of their lives. That one,

larky, long in the leg, red-bearded, he
will not come back. Already his grave
is marked, he will not see his grandchildren.
The young one, who knows the flight

of lark and pipit and holds their bald nestlings
within his hands, will fall apprentice
to a butcher. He will run screaming
from the slaughterhouse, his eyes full

of hacked red meat, the round cries
of animals will follow him all his roads.
He will walk through the dark lots,
through brutal labour in furnaces,

through human betrayal. His sisters
will curb their thin tongues, laugh
bitterly and in secret; endure. They will
never return. It is I who recall their ghosts

to the house under the hill, their
wavering dust so frail it does not stir
the powder of the roads. It is I
who people the lanes of homecoming

and build the fallen chimneys stone by stone
so the doused fires will carry the echoes
of old warmth, and the fields hear more
than the hawk's voice, and the silence after.

A Sea in the Desert

1

A little sea
in the night
ran its inch of tide
about the bole of the peach tree,

hesitated,
came fawning to my door,
cringed,
fell away.

Its small crests,
Its ebb,
broke my sleep.

2

A little sea
was running in the desert.
It came in
under the edges of the breeze,
a true sea,
sharpening the air with salt,
filling hourly through the night.

It remembered white ships,
    clippers out of China
        freighted with tea and roses,
            sea-swans
    holding gales in their wings,
storms off the coast of fragrant Spain, snarling.

        It hurled
    against my walls
        its gathering whips and drums,
            dropped away,
its throat rattling with pebbles.

3

I got up,
    opened my door
        to this unbelievable sea.

        My yard was lit by silent moonlight.
Parched grasshoppers chirrupped in the ditches.

4

But still the sea broke
    on the beaches of my ears.

My skull was a shell
holding the noisy tides
Pouring unseen over the desert.

5

A man is moon to his own sea –
he draws it after him,
like a dog it follows him
the days of his life.

All that night I heard the sea make
and ebb, a sea formed
of grains of remembered oceans,
fed by rains and rivers

of days I had finished with.
It carried old sticks in its mouth.
In the morning a tide's detritus,
twigs, small round stones, a can,

lay in uneven lines
on the charred grass.

6

A hermit thrush sings for me
in dry arroyos its liquid note.
I have heard in the desert
unrecognised birds, charmers,

lift up their single whistles,
long separated, distant,
purified by distance, among
the grassless dunes.

I have thought them calling me.
I have heard the voices
of an invisible sea
whispering with boys'

voices, heard in its dry waves
the pattering of boys' feet
through the built canyons
of the past. I have heard

such singing. The mocking-bird
has sung for me. Each day
the waters of that sea
are rising blindly to the full.

Borders

(i.m. John Ormond, died May 4th 1990)

The border I knew best was halfway over
the bridge between the town and Breconshire.
Beneath,
          the river's neutral water
moved on
          to other boundaries.

I walked the bridge each Saturday, stopped
at a guessed measure,
lived a moment in adventurous limbo.
Did I stand on air then, invisibly
taken to some unknown world, some nowhere?
Where was I then? I was whole
but felt an unseen line
divide me, send my strong half forward,
keep my other timidly at home.

I have always lived that way,
crossed borders resolutely
while looking over my shoulder.

Not long ago
driving in America
in high cold desert country below the Rockies,
I saw at the roadside
parked on an acre open as the moon,

a ring of shabby cars
old Chevies and Caddies,
some prosperous trucks.
The Indians were showing on folding tables
their ceremonial silver, heavy necklaces, rich
with turquoise and hammered squash-blossom,
                                                            oval
silver bangles.

                        Navajo and Zuni,
old tribes, hardy and skilled.
They stood behind their work in the flat wind,
not smiling.
I love the things they make,
haggled for a buckle for my belt,
silver, a design
rayed liked the cold sun,
and, walking away, saw
cut into the concrete
the meeting place of four states.
Crouched there, I placed a foot in Utah,
a foot in Arizona, my palms flat
in the dust of Colorado and New Mexico.

Restless as dust, scattered.

A man I knew, my old friend,
moved out as I did, but returned,
followed his eyes and crossed the borders

into his own country. When he left,
it was to see his place from a distance
and peacefully go home. The world grew small
for him, to one country, a city, a house.

His mother, calmly and nobly dying,
asked on her last day for champagne
which she had never tasted. She wet her lips,
and in the evening called into her room
someone unseen. 'Who would have thought it,'
she said, very clearly, and crossed the border
for which all others are a preparation.

And Sally Taylor, her mother dying in the next room,
heard women's voices, young and laughing,
come in to fetch the old lady.
Border, boundary, threshold, door –
Orpheus moved either way, the living and the dead
were parted by a thin reflection
he simply walked through. But who can follow?

For all the boundaries I have crossed, flown over,
knowingly, unknowingly, I have no answers;
but sit in the afternoon sun, under mountains
where stale snow clings in shadowy patches,
remember my friend, how he had sung,
hope he is still singing.

His Father, Singing

My father sang for himself,
out of sadness and poverty;
perhaps from happiness,
but I'm not sure of that.

He sang in the garden,
quietly, a quiet voice
near his wallflowers
which of all plants

he loved most, calling them
gillyflowers, a name
learned from his mother.
His songs came from a time

before my time, his boy's
life among musical brothers,
keeping pigeons, red and blue
checkers, had a racing cycle

with bamboo wheels. More often
he sang the songs he'd learned,
still a boy, up to his knees
in French mud, those dying songs.

He sang for us once only,
our mother away from the house,

the lamp lit, and I reading,
seven years old, already bookish,

at the scrubbed table.
My brother cried from his crib
in the small bedroom, teething,
a peremptory squall, then a long

wail. My father lifted from
the sheets his peevish child,
red-faced, feverish, carried
him down in a wool shawl

and in the kitchen, holding
the child close, began to sing.
Quietly, of course, and swaying
rhythmically from foot to foot,

he rocked the sobbing boy.
I saw my brother's head,
his puckered face, fall
on my father's chest. His crying

died away, and I
read on. It was my father's
singing brought my head up.
His little wordless lullabies

had gone, and what he sang
above his baby's sleep
was never meant
for any infant's comfort.

He stood in the bleak kitchen,
the stern, young man, my father.
For the first time raised
his voice, in pain and anger

sang. I did not know his song
nor why he sang it. But stood
in fright, knowing it important,
and someone should be listening.

A Visitation of Welshmen

This morning he takes the car up the hill
and parks at the corner of Fourth and Tenth.
It is early, but dawn runners in their sweats
have all jogged home; journeymen, their pickups
heavy
with metal toolboxes, with shovels and pickaxes
and coils of electrical wire, have been an hour
at work. Business people and the professionally
suited
have not moved from their breakfasts. It is between
purposeful times. He walks along the old road
as it attends the river or turns for some ancient
reason
from the river's voice. Cottonwoods hang over him.
The runnels are full of their white tufts.

He is happy under the branches, stepping
in dappled light. In Slindon Woods, years ago,
he knew a tree which held beneath its tent
a clearly defined warm air, always warm and still,
even in winter. That was a small beech tree, young
in a company of veterans. And there were other
trees,
untidy evergreens, restless and irritable, without
comfort. He did not have to think then of such
things,
to recognise a wych elm, to mark how a wild briar

thrust its simple blossoms among the hawthorns.
Here he has to learn by conscious observation
the trees he passes under. He forgets their names.

(But – an old superstition in his country –
he always stations at his gate a pair of rowans,
red berried, an arboreal safeguard against evil.)
The sequoia, the bristlecone pine, the ponderosa
will not stand in the landscapes of his dreams,
taller
though they may grow, nor the honey locust and
the northern catalpa. So it is surprising that there
come into his mind in this alien country, almost
as if he had never left them, men of his family
he has not thought of for many years. Dead men,
all of them, uncles and great-uncles, his grandfather,
so long dead he could not recall the old man's face,

Yet here they smile at him in their living lines,
familiar as his own hands. 'I saw you,' says
his grandfather, 'at Bethel Chapel door, penniless
outside the penny concert. A little boy, tense,
standing straight up, determined, with another
little boy.
"Let him in, Dadcu," you said, "Let him in, he's
my pal."
I liked that. I knew then you'd go a long way.'
He stands among the approving ghosts, disturbed.
'I don't remember,' he says. 'Oh, we do,'

his uncle Jacko says, 'It's not enough you could read
before you could walk. We've had to listen
all these years to stories of how wonderful you were.

You're Dad's favourite. But you have come a long
way.'
Smiling and nodding. 'The promised land,' says
Willie John,
his dancing cousin, amused and tolerantly mocking.
'This is a generous country,' he replies, 'Great cities,
deserts no man has ever walked. An abounding
country.'
But even as he speaks, it sounds like an apology.
Only death could have pulled these stubborn
shadows
out of their sour fields, the poor streets strung
among
coaltips. There's not a man among them would have
walked to Birmingham to the factories, or sailed
out of Aberaeron harbour with a cargo of salt for
Liverpool.
Certainly not a man had walked the deep seaways
and,

thinking he'd seen a ghost, had found his brother
in the streets of Valparaiso. 'You've a good place
here,
right enough,' Willie John says, 'Tribal. Utes, Zunis,

mountainmen, Mormons. We Joneses would fit
right in.
You've chosen well.' Their laughter is all around
him,
kind and fond, and he laughs with them, all
distance gone,
his daily questions calmed and rested. A small wind
from the world startles him alert. His warm ghosts
are going home. 'All's well,' his grandfather says,
his voice
not even a whisper. It sounded like "All's well".
He walks
in the dust as if he is young and the sun not yet a
burden.
Traffic is moving over the river bridge; but a serene,
momentary radiance which is his alone and nothing

to do with the morning is showing him a brief
eternity.
He has plenty of time. Three calling boys at the
river's edge
throw down their bikes. Thinking of six pound
trout,
they tie their hopeful lures, reel out their lines and
cast
into the lucent morning. 'All's well,' he says, 'all's
well'.

Shaving

Earlier, when Barry had left the house to go to the game, an overnight frost had still been thick on the roads, but the brisk April sun had soon dispersed it, and now he could feel the spring warmth on his back through the thick tweed of his coat. His left arm was beginning to stiffen up where he'd jarred it in a tackle, but it was nothing serious. He flexed his shoulders against the tightness of his jacket and was surprised again by the unexpected weight of his muscles, the thickening strength of his body. A few years back, he thought, he had been a small, unimportant boy, one of a swarming gang laughing and jostling to school, hardly aware that he possessed an identity. But time had transformed him. He walked solidly now, and often alone. He was tall, strongly made, his hands and feet were adult and heavy, the rooms in which all his life he'd moved had grown too small for him. Sometimes a devouring restlessness drove him from the house to walk long distances in the dark. He hardly understood how it had happened. Amused and quiet, he walked the High Street among the morning shoppers.

He saw Jackie Bevan across the road and remembered how, when they were both six years old, Jackie had swallowed a pin. The flustered teachers had clucked about Jackie as he stood there, bawling, cheeks awash with tears, his nose wet. But now Jackie was tall and suave, his thick, pale hair sleekly tailored, his grey suit enviable. He was talking to a girl as golden as a daffodil. 'Hey, hey!' called Jackie. 'How's the athlete, how's Barry boy?'

He waved a graceful hand at Barry.

'Come and talk to Sue,' he said.

Barry shifted his bag to his left hand and walked over, forming in his mind the answers he'd make to Jackie's questions.

'Did we win?' Jackie asked. 'Was the old Barry Stanford magic in glittering evidence yet once more this morning? Were the invaders sent hunched and silent back to their hovels in the hills? What was the score? Give us an epic account, Barry, without modesty or delay. This is Sue, by the way.'

'I've seen you about,' the girl said.

'You could hardly miss him,' said Jackie. 'Four men, roped together, spent a week climbing him – they thought he was Everest. He ought to carry a warning beacon, he's a danger to aircraft.'

'Silly,' said the girl, smiling at Jackie. 'He's not much taller than you are.'

She had a nice voice too.

'We won,' Barry said. 'Seventeen points to three, and it was a good game. The ground was hard, though.'

He could think of nothing else to say.

'Let's all go for a frivolous cup of coffee,' Jackie

said. 'Let's celebrate your safe return from the rough fields of victory. We could pour libations all over the floor for you.'

'I don't think so,' Barry said. 'Thanks. I'll go straight home.'

'Okay,' said Jackie, rocking on his heels so that the sun could shine on his smile. 'How's your father?'

'No better,' Barry said. 'He's not going to get better.'

'Yes, well,' said Jackie, serious and uncomfortable, 'tell him my mother and father ask about him.'

'I will,' Barry promised. 'He'll be pleased.'

Barry dropped the bag in the front hall and moved into the room which had been the dining room until his father's illness. His father lay in the white bed, his long body gaunt, his still head scarcely denting the pillow. He seemed asleep, thin blue lids covering his eyes, but when Barry turned away he spoke.

'Hello, son,' he said. 'Did you win?'

His voice was a dry rustling, hardly louder than the breath which carried it. Its sound moved Barry to a compassion that almost unmanned him, but he stepped close to the bed and looked down at the dying man.

'Yes,' he said. 'We won fairly easily. It was a good game.'

His father lay with his eyes closed, inert, his breath irregular and shallow.

'Did you score?' he asked.

'Twice,' Barry said. 'I had a try in each half.'

He thought of the easy certainty with which he'd caught the ball before his second try; casually, almost arrogantly he had taken it on the tips of his fingers, on his full burst for the line, breaking the fullback's tackle. Nobody could have stopped him. But watching his father's weakness he felt humble and ashamed, as if the morning's game, its urgency and effort, was not worth talking about. His father's face, fine-skinned and pallid, carried a dark stubble of beard, almost a week's growth, and his obstinate, strong hair stuck out over his brow.

'Good,' said his father, after a long pause. 'I'm glad it was a good game.'

Barry's mother bustled about the kitchen, a tempest of orderly energy.

'Your father's not well,' she said. 'He's down today, feels depressed. He's a particular man, your father. He feels dirty with all that beard on him.'

She slammed shut the stove door.

'Mr Cleaver was supposed to come up and shave him' she said, 'and that was three days ago. Little things have always worried your father, every detail must be perfect for him.'

Barry filled a glass with milk from the refrigerator. He was very thirsty.

'I'll shave him,' he said.

His mother stopped, her head on one side.

'Do you think you can?' she asked. 'He'd like it if you can.'

'I can do it,' Barry said.

He washed his hands as carefully as a surgeon. His father's razor was in a blue leather case, hinged at the broad edge and with one hinge broken. Barry unfastened the clasp and took out the razor. It had not been properly cleaned after its last use and lather had stiffened into hard yellow rectangles between the teeth of the guard. There were water-shaped rust stains, brown as chocolate, on the surface of the blade. Barry removed it, throwing it in the waste bin. He washed the razor until it glistened, and dried it on a soft towel, polishing the thin handle, rubbing its metal head to a glittering shine. He took a new blade from its waxed envelope, the paper clinging to the thin metal. The blade was smooth and flexible to the touch, the little angles of its cutting clearly defined. Barry slotted it into the grip of the razor, making it snug and tight in the head.

The shaving soap, hard, white, richly aromatic, was kept in a wooden bowl. Its scent was immediately evocative and Barry could almost see his father in the days of his health, standing before his mirror, thick white lather on his face and neck. As a little boy Barry had loved the generous perfume of the soap, had waited for his father to lift the razor to his face, for one careful stroke to take away the suds in a clean revelation of the skin. Then his father would renew the lather with a few sweeps of his brush, one with an ivory handle and the bristles worn, which he still used.

His father's shaving mug was a thick cup, plain and serviceable. A gold line ran outside the rim of the cup, another inside, just below the lip. Its handle was large and sturdy, and the face of the mug carried a portrait of the young Queen Elizabeth II, circled by a wreath of leaves, oak perhaps, or laurel. A lion and unicorn balanced precariously on a scroll above her crowned head, and the Union Jack, the Royal Standard, and other flags were furled on each side of the portrait. And beneath it all, in small black letters, ran the legend: 'Coronation June 2nd 1953'. The cup was much older than Barry. A pattern of faint translucent cracks, fine as a web, had worked itself haphazardly, invisibly almost, through the white glaze. Inside, on the bottom, a few dark bristles were lying, loose and dry. Barry shook them out, then held the cup in his hand, feeling its solidness. Then he washed it ferociously, until it was clinically clean.

Methodically he set everything on a tray, razor, soap, brush, towels. Testing the hot water with a finger, he filled the mug and put that, too, on the tray. His care was absorbed, ritualistic. Satisfied that his preparations were complete, he went downstairs, carrying the tray with one hand.

His father was waiting for him. Barry set the tray on a bedside table and bent over his father, sliding an arm under the man's thin shoulders, lifting him without effort so that he sat against the high pillows.

'By God, you're strong,' his father said. He was as breathless as if he'd been running.

'So are you,' said Barry.

'I was,' his father said. 'I used to be strong once.' He sat exhausted against the pillows.

'We'll wait a bit,' Barry said.

'You could have used your electric razor,' his father said. 'I expected that.'

'You wouldn't like it,' Barry said. 'You'll get a closer shave this way.'

He placed the large towel about his father's shoulders.

'Now,' he said, smiling down.

The water was hot in the thick cup. Barry wet the brush and worked up the lather. Gently he built up a covering of soft foam on the man's chin, on his cheeks and his stark cheekbones.

'You're using a lot of soap,' his father said.

'Not too much,' Barry said. 'You've got a lot of beard.'

His father lay there quietly, his wasted arms at his sides.

'It's comforting,' he said. 'You'd be surprised how comforting it is.'

Barry took up the razor, weighing it in his hand, rehearsing the angle at which he'd use it. He felt confident.

'If you have prayers to say . . . ' he said.

'I've said a lot of prayers,' his father answered.

Barry leaned over and placed the razor delicately on the clean line near the ear where the long hair ended. He held the razor in the tips of his fingers and drew the blade sweetly through the lather. The new edge moved light as a touch over the hardness of the upper jaw and down to the angle of the chin, sliding away the bristles so easily that Barry could not feel their release. He sighed as he shook the razor in the hot water, washing away the soap.

'How's it going?' his father asked.

'No problem,' Barry said. 'You needn't worry.'

It was as if he had never known what his father really looked like. He was discovering under his hands the clear bones of the face and head, they became sharp and recognisable under his fingers. When he moved his father's face a gentle inch to one side, he touched with his fingers the frail temples, the blue veins of his father's life. With infinite and meticulous care he took away the hair from his father's face.

'Now for your neck,' he said. 'We might as well do the job properly.'

'You've got good hands,' his father said. 'You can trust those hands, they won't let you down.'

Barry cradled his father's head in the crook of his left arm, so that the man could tilt back his head, exposing the throat. He brushed fresh lather under the chin and into the hollows alongside the stretched tendons. His father's throat was fleshless and vulnerable, his head was a hard weight on the boy's arm. Barry was filled with unreasoning protective love. He lifted the razor and began to shave.

'You don't have to worry,' he said. 'Not at all. Not about anything.'

He held his father in the bend of his strong arm and they looked at each other. Their heads were very close.

'How old are you?' his father said.

'Seventeen,' Barry said. 'Near enough seventeen.'

'You're young,' his father said, 'to have this happen.'

'Not too young,' Barry said. 'I'm bigger than most men.'

'I think you are,' his father said.

He leaned his head tiredly against the boy's shoulder. He was without strength, his face was cold and smooth. He had let go all his authority, handed it over. He lay back on his pillow, knowing his weakness and his mortality, and looked at his son with wonder, with a curious humble pride.

'I won't worry then,' he said. 'About anything.'

'There's no need,' Barry said. 'Why should you worry?'

He wiped his father's face clean of all soap with a damp towel. The smell of illness was everywhere, overpowering even the perfumed lather. Barry settled his father down and took away the shaving tools, putting them by with the same ceremonial precision with which he'd prepared them: the cleaned and glittering razor in its broken case; the soap, its bowl wiped and dried, on the shelf between the brush and the coronation mug; all free of taint. He washed his hands and scrubbed his nails. His hands were firm and broad, pink after their scrubbing. The fingers were short and strong, the little fingers slightly crooked, and soft dark hair grew on the backs of his hands and his fingers just above the knuckles. Not long ago they had been small bare hands, not very long ago.

Barry opened wide the bathroom window. Already, although it was not yet two o'clock, the sun was retreating and people were moving briskly, wrapped in their heavy coats against the cold that was to come. But now the window was full in the beam of the dying sunlight, and Barry stood there, illuminated in its golden warmth for a whole minute, knowing it would soon be gone.

For further reading

Poetry

The Loud Winter (Triskel Press, 1967)
Finding Gold (Chatto and Windus, 1967)
Ransoms (Chatto and Windus, 1970)
Mountains Polecats Pheasants (Chatto and Windus, 1974)
Merlin and the Snake's Egg (The Viking Press, 1978)
Water Voices (Chatto and Windus, 1980)
Walking the White Fields (Little, Brown and Co., 1980)
Selected Poems (Poetry Wales Press, 1986)
Sequences (Peregrine Smith Books, 1988)
Norris's Ark (The Tidal Press, 1988)
A Sea in the Desert (Seren, 1989)
The Sonnets to Orpheus by Rainer Maria Rilke, trans. with Alan Keele (Camden House, 1989)
The Duino Elegies by Rainer Maria Rilke, trans. with Alan Keele (Camden House, 1993)
Collected Poems (Seren, 1996)
Winter Wreath, poems (Tryst Press, 1998)

Prose

Sliding (Charles Scribner's Sons, 1976)
The Girl from Cardigan (Seren, 1988)
Collected Stories (Seren, 1996)
Collected Stories (Seren, reprinted 1997)
Albert and the Angels (Farrar, Strauss and Giroux, 2000)

Literary Criticism

James A. Davies, *Leslie Norris* in the *Writers of Wales* series (University of Wales Press, 1991)
Eugene England and Peter Makuk, *An Open World* (Camden House, 1994)

Leslie Norris has contributed a monograph on Glyn Jones to the *Writers of Wales* series (1973; revised edn. 1997)

Images of Wales

The Corgi Series covers, no.13
'The Adventurer' by John Elwyn, 1954; oil on canvas, 20x25 inches; (by kind permission of Robert Meyrick, School of Art, University of Wales, Aberystwyth)

John Elwyn (1916-97) was a native of Adpar, Newcastle Emlyn, Cardiganshire, and from 1953 to 1976 taught at the School of Art in Winchester. He painted, for the most part, scenes of rural life in west Wales and, in 1956, was awarded the Gold Medal for Fine Art by the National Eisteddfod.